MARK FERGUSON

101 House Flipping Tips

Insider's Guide to Maximizing Profits and Avoiding Costly Mistakes

First published by InvestFourMore 2019

Copyright © 2019 by Mark Ferguson

All rights reserved. No part of this publication may be reproduced, stored or transmitted in any form or by any means, electronic, mechanical, photocopying, recording, scanning, or otherwise without written permission from the publisher. It is illegal to copy this book, post it to a website, or distribute it by any other means without permission.

Mark Ferguson has no responsibility for the persistence or accuracy of URLs for external or third-party Internet Websites referred to in this publication and does not guarantee that any content on such Websites is, or will remain, accurate or appropriate.

Designations used by companies to distinguish their products are often claimed as trademarks. All brand names and product names used in this book and on its cover are trade names, service marks, trademarks and registered trademarks of their respective owners. The publishers and the book are not associated with any product or vendor mentioned in this book. None of the companies referenced within the book have endorsed the book.

First edition

Editing by Greg Helmerick

This book was professionally typeset on Reedsy.
Find out more at reedsy.com

This book is dedicated to everyone who has ever thought about flipping homes and wants to know how the business really works.

Contents

Foreword	v
Introduction	1
Never Price a House Flip Too High	3
Stick With Neutral Colors to Get the Most Money	5
Getting Loans on Flips Usually Results in Higher Profits…	7
Is the 70 Percent Rule a Good Way to Judge a Flip?	9
Knowing Market Value Is the Most Important Part of Flipping…	12
High-End Houses Are Cool but Expensive to Flip! Be Very…	13
Television Shows Will Not Help You Learn to Flip Houses	14
Great Contractors Are the Key to a Profitable Flipping…	15
Don't Ever Open a Freezer or Fridge at House You Just Bought	17
There Is No Need to Spend $40,000 on a House Flipping Course…	18
Time is Money! It Can Cost From $50 to $100 a Day to Own a…	20
There Will Be Rough Times. You Cannot Give Up	22
Leave Your Emotions at the Door	23
Do Not Underestimate the Cost of a Trash-out or Eviction	25
Always Get the HVAC Checked Out No Matter How New It Is	27
Waiving the Inspection Is a Great Way to Get More Deals	28
Home Depot and Lowes Have Great Programs for Flippers	29
While Neutral Colors Sell, You Do Not Have to Be Boring	31
Selling a House in the Winter Is Not Always Bad	32
Being Too Trendy Can Make It Tougher to Sell a Flip	33
Check Your Properties at Least Once a Week	34
Making a House Perfect Is Not Possible	36
The Older a Home Is, the More Problems it Can Have	37
Do Not Work on the Houses Yourself	38

Do Not Discount the MLS Even in a Hot Market	40
Never Trust a Wholesaler's Numbers. Verify Everything.	42
Make Sure You Are Following All EPA Guidelines	44
Some Houses Are Not Worth Flipping No Matter What the Price	45
Busy Roads Can Make a House a Nightmare to Sell	47
Buying a House Occupied by Tenants Can be a Great Way to Get...	48
Prep the Listing Agent before Sending in a Low Offer	50
Always Check for Flood Zones before Buying a House	52
Make Sure All Broken Windows and Doors Are Boarded or Fixed	54
Beware of the Fake Private-Money Lender!	55
The 90-Day Flip Rule Can Make it Tough to Sell Fast	56
Flips Are More of a Job Than an Investment	57
Remember to Take Time off and Enjoy What Your Hard Work...	58
You Do Not Have to Buy a Foreclosure to Get a Good Deal	59
Pre-Inspecting a Home Can Help with the Scope of Work for...	60
You Don't Get to Keep Everything in a House When You Buy it;...	61
Ask the Title Company For a Hold Open Policy to Save Money	62
Right Now is the Perfect Time of Year to Sell	63
Beware of Structural Problems	64
Simple Touches Can Add a Lot of Value	66
Restoring is Different than Renovating	67
Small Houses May Not Sell for as Much, But They Are Much...	68
Don't Ever Assume Prices Will Go Up, Leading to a Profit	69
Unique Homes Are Interesting but Often Hard to Sell	70
Design Choices Can be Region Specific; Study Your Market	71
Laminate Flooring Is One Way to Save Money	72
Never Pay Contractors in Full until the Job Is Done	73
Try Not to Pay a Contractor Too Much Money Upfront	74
No Matter How it Looks in the Movie, Don't Slide Down a...	75
The More Subcontractors You Can Find the Better	76
Be Careful Not to Get Caught Up in Bidding Wars	77
Too Many Low-Ball Offers Can Be a Bad Thing	78
Being a Real Estate Agent Can Be a Huge Advantage	79

Two Houses on the Same Lot Do Not Equal Twice the Value	80
Real Private Money Is from People You Know	81
Always Get Everything in Writing when Working with a Partner	82
Meth Houses Can be a Disaster	83
Always Use a Real Estate Agent to Sell a Flip	84
Local Banks Can Be a Great Source of Funding	85
Always Make Sure the Jobsite is Safe	86
Saving Money, Not Spending It, Is the Key to Flipping	87
Make Sure You Check the Heat in the Winter	88
Don't Fudge the Numbers to Make a Deal Work	89
A Team is a Wonderful Thing	90
Paying for Materials Can Be a Great Way to Save Money	91
Text2Confirm is Awesome	92
A Line of Credit Is a Great Way to Fund Flips	93
Beware of Haunted Houses and Dead People	94
Always Get a W9 From Your Contractors and Subs	95
Why Won't My Flip Sell?	96
Take videos and Pictures of Every Flip	97
The Key to a Successful Flipping Business is Doing More than...	98
Flipping Really Cheap Houses Can Be Tough	99
House Flipping Will Not Fix Your Money Problems	100
An Owner-Occupant Flip Can Net Big, Tax-Free Profits	101
It Is Really Tough to Flip Houses in a Different Market	102
Insurance Can Be Expensive...and Tough to Find	103
Goals Are Almost as Important as the Work	104
When Do You Need a Building Permit?	105
Do Not Be Scared of Your Contractor	106
Make Sure the Doors and Windows Are Intact in the Winter	107
You Can Flip Houses in Any Market	108
I Don't Care About the Schools or Crime	109
Lowes and Home Depot Offer Awesome Military Discounts Year...	110
The Average Purchase Price of My Flips Is $200,000 and My...	111
Save Time by Not Attending the Closing with the Buyers or...	112

Water Is One of the Most Destructive Forces	113
Buying in Bulk Can Be a Great Way to Save Money	114
Is There a Best Time of the Week to List a House?	115
Help Appraisers Out!	116
FHA Appraisals Stick with a Home for 6 Months	117
Don't Forget to Shovel the Walks and Mow the Grass	118
It Is Possible to Challenge a Low Appraisal	119
You Do Not Have to Completely Remodel Every Flip	120
The First Offer You Get Is Often the Best Offer	121
Flipping with a Partner Is One Way to Flip with No Money	122
Conclusion	123
About Mark Ferguson	124
Want to Learn More?	126

Foreword

In keeping with the style of the book, I wanted this foreword to cover 5 tips to understanding Mark and his business model (the good, the bad, and the quirky). I have worked for Mark for almost 10 years now and feel like I have a pretty good understanding of the day-to-day aspects of his business. I hope these 5 short tips give you a little insight into the Mark that many don't get the privilege of knowing.

1. Many of us who work with mark like to label some of the worst houses we see as "Mark Ferguson Specials." Mark has made turning some of the absolute biggest eye sores into great livable homes that many people are excited to buy one of his specialties. He has also made an absolute mess of some of these houses and regretted ever taking them on. Approach a "Mark Ferguson Special" carefully and know there's a pretty equal chance of it going great or going absolutely horribly.
2. If you ever meet Mark in person and are at a loss for topics to talk about, some safe suggestions other than real estate are cars (the older and more exotic the better), bad movies with stupid humor (think Zoolander, Stepbrothers, etc..), or the weather (the guy loves a good weather radar map).
3. Be flexible. Mark likes to brag about all the systems he has in place to find contractors, keep jobs running, etc. And for some things, he does have great systems. But for other things, he has no systems at all and is very fly by the seat of his pants. The lesson here is to have some structure but also be open to putting the systems aside and just going with the flow of things.
4. Think outside the box. Mark has flipped through markets that most

can't flip through...and made a profit. Mark has cash-flowing rentals in a market where most are not cash flowing at all. Mark has sold 200+ houses a year when most agents were hanging up their licenses due to low sales numbers. When one aspect of his business slows down or he isn't getting the results he is looking for, he thinks outside of the box and finds a new niche to make his numbers and business work.

5. Be willing to put in the work. Mark hasn't written 10+ books, flipped over 200 houses, or become as successful as he is by not putting in the work. If you think all he does is drive around in his fancy cars and play golf, you are very wrong. If you want to be successful and have a list of accomplishments like he does, you must be willing to put in the work!

1

Introduction

I have written a number of books on real estate, and even a fiction book about buying a house for the first time. In those books, I go to great lengths and into great detail to explain everything I can.

This book is completely different.

I wrote this book to give people quick tips that they can easily reference over and over. You don't have to search through hundreds of pages of text to find one simple concept. That said, if you want to read hundreds of pages and detailed information about real estate, please check out my other books.

I felt I was qualified to write this book since I have flipped over 180 houses and counting. I flipped 26 houses last year. I love the business, and I love finding deals. Getting started can be stressful and tough, but once you learn the business, it is tough to ever stop. Not only is it fun, but it is exciting! We are always learning something new, even after 17 years in the business. I have a lot of experience, but I still don't know everything...and never will.

This book is self explanatory. I provide 101 tips for flipping houses and expand on each tip. I chose the most important tips I could to help people be successful in this business. If anyone has questions, let me know!

Mark@investfourmore.com. I love getting emails from people and doing my best to point them in the right direction or help anyway I can.

Not only have I written many other books, fiction and non-fiction, on flipping, rentals, being an agent, mindset, and negotiations, but I also have some coaching available. This is not the $30,000 coaching you may have run into with other flipper programs. I keep my programs as affordable as possible to help as many people as I can.

We show almost all of our flips on the InvestFourMore YouTube channel and I post daily on the InvestFourMore Instagram and Facebook pages.

I hope you enjoy the book! I know I enjoyed creating it.

2

Never Price a House Flip Too High

One of the most important parts of selling a house is pricing it right. This is one reason why real estate agents are so important. Good agents are experts at valuing and pricing homes. Some people may not think the price is that important because if you price too low, you will start a bidding war, and if you price too high, people will offer lower. This is not the case!

If you price a home too high, many people will not even go see it. Buyers have an expectation that houses they can buy will be priced close to market value. They do not assume that the seller is willing to negotiate a lot. If you price a home too high, it will most likely sit on the market with very few showings. Once it has been on the market a certain amount of time, people will start to wonder what is wrong with it. "If it has not sold yet, it must be a bad house!" Even if you drop the price, buyers will still see it has been on the market an extended period of time and wonder what is wrong if it has not sold yet. Pricing a home too high almost always results in a house selling for less than it could have if it was priced right.

Please remember that the market does not care how much you spent fixing up the home or how far over budget you went. They care about what they think it is worth compared to other sales in the area.

If you price a home too low, you also usually lose out on money. Yes, it is true that low-priced homes sometimes get multiple offers, but not always. When you price a home too low, you often get one or two buyers who have been waiting for the right home. You also will get investors (like us) waiting for a great deal. The investors may even low-ball the price even more to get a deal (I would). The buyers who have been waiting for a home to come up will likely offer full price. Some may offer a little more, but not always. Many buyers do not want to get in a "bidding war" and may not even offer if they know they have to compete with others. There is also a chance you may only get one offer and no one else is ready to commit right away. If you had priced the home right, the buyers most likely would pay what you are asking, but since you priced it low, they still pay what you are asking, and it costs you money.

Another problem with pricing a home low is it gives appraisers another excuse to come in low with their value. They often do not like to value a home at more than list price even if they know there are multiple offers.

Price a home right, and it will pay off. Price a home wrong, and it can cost you 10 percent or more of the sales price.

3

Stick With Neutral Colors to Get the Most Money

A lot of people like to get creative and "Joanna Gaines" a house. They want trendy colors everywhere with 14 accent walls. A few people may love what you do with the house, but most people will not. Everyone has different tastes, but most people won't mind a house that is painted with neutral colors.

People are also very emotionally driven when they buy a house. They may not even realize why they like a home, but the "feel" and paint can affect them greatly. Colors that are too dark, too light, or different from what most people are used to can make them dislike a home even though they may not know that is what is causing their dislike.

A lot of flippers may think that if the colors don't work for people, they can just repaint it themselves. For one thing, most people who are buying a house that has been flipped do not want to do any work to the home. Painting a house is also difficult. They have to wait to move in, may not know any painters, and may not want to go through the hassle of picking colors themselves.

An entire house painted in one neutral color (usually a beige, off white, or grey) is appealing to most people. When you appeal to the most people, you sell your house for the most money. It is much easier for the buyer to paint one accent wall if they want to spice things up.

We stay neutral with almost all of or design choices.

4

Getting Loans on Flips Usually Results in Higher Profits than Paying All Cash

A lot of people ask me why I don't pay cash for my flips at this point in my career. They assume that I would make more money because I would not pay interest or points on the loan. The fact is, I make more money using leverage or loans.

Flipping a house is really expensive. I am paying about $200,000 on average for a flip in my market. Then, I spend $30,000 on the repairs and another $5,000 to $15,000 on the carrying costs and financing costs.

If I paid all cash for that house, I would have at least $235,000 into it. If I were to get a loan, I could reduce the amount I have into the property to $20,000 to $75,000 depending on the type of financing I use. I have from 12 to 22 flips going at once. Keeping that many flips working takes a lot of money, even when I use financing. It takes even more if I were to use all cash. I would have from $2,800,000 to $5,100,000 in cash into my flips. I don't have that much cash lying around, nor would I want that much cash invested in my flips. I would rather have it in rentals.

By using loans, I have from $500,000 to $1,000,000 in cash invested in my flips. That is still a lot of money, but much less than if I was using all cash. I can basically do three to four times as many flips using loans as I could just paying cash.

We also have to look at my financing costs. I use private money, bank money, and once in awhile, hard money. I can pay from $5,000 to $10,000 in financing costs on that house I buy for $200,000. People assume I would make more money on my flips if I did not have those financing costs and paid cash. That is true on one flip, but I can do three to four times more flips with loans. My average profit on a house flip is over $30,000 with financing costs. It may be $40,000 without.

So I could make $40,000 on one flip by paying cash, or I could make $90,000 to $120,000 on three or four flips by using loans. I would rather make $90,000.

5

Is the 70 Percent Rule a Good Way to Judge a Flip?

The 70 percent rule is widely used to judge if a home can be flipped. The 70 percent rule goes like this:

The purchase price of the home should be 70 percent of the ARV (After Repaired Value) minus any repairs needed. For example, if a house would be worth $280,000 after it is repaired, and it needs $30,000 in work, you should pay $166,000 for the house.

($280,000 x .7) minus $30,000 = $166,000

If a house is worth $150,000 after the repairs and it needs $20,000 in work, you should pay $85,000.

($150,000 x .7) minus $20,000 = $85,000

The problem with this equation for me is that in the more expensive example, the difference between the purchase price and the selling price is $114,000, but in the lower-priced example, it is $65,000. The more expensive the home is, the harder it is to meet the 70 percent rule. I used to have no problem hitting that rule when our prices were lower, but now I almost never do.

Yes, the costs increase with a more expensive home. The selling costs, financing costs, and carrying costs are higher. But, they are not that much higher.

Sales price: $280,000
  Repairs: $30,000
  Other costs: $18,000
  Buying price: $166,000
  Profit: $66,000

Sales price: $150,000
  Repairs: $20,000
  other costs: $12,000
  Buying Price: $85,000
  Profit: $33,000

With the 70 percent rule, the more-expensive house makes twice as much money. That make sense because the rule is based on percentages. I would love to make $66,000 on each flip I do, but the market rarely, if ever, allows that high of a profit margin. There is too much competition, and sellers are too savvy.

I would be happy to make $30,000 on the upper example, which means I would be buying the house for $200,000, not $166,000. At that price, I would be paying 80 percent of the ARV. However, on lower-dollar values, I may want to buy at even less than 70 percent.

Sales price: $100,000
  Repairs: $20,000
  Other costs: $10,000
  Buying price: $50,000

IS THE 70 PERCENT RULE A GOOD WAY TO JUDGE A FLIP?

Profit: $20,000

A $20,000 profit is not usually good enough for me, so I would want to buy that property at 65 percent of the ARV or less. This is why I do not like to use rules when I invest in real estate. There are too many rule variables to keep track of.

Something else to consider is that property taxes, insurance, financing costs, and repairs are different on every deal. The 70 percent rule does not account for any of that. The 70 percent rule also does not account for large remodels versus small remodels. I want a much larger profit margin on a large remodel than I do on a small remodel.

One more thing to consider is that I am a real estate agent. My costs to sell and buy are often much less than non agents. The 70 percent rule will not account for that either.

I think the best way to calculate the profit on a flip is to write out all the costs on every deal. It really is not that hard.

6

Knowing Market Value Is the Most Important Part of Flipping Houses

A lot of people ask me how I know what a house will be worth once it sells. This question frustrates me a little because it is possibly the most important thing an investor can know. If you have no idea what market values are, you should not be flipping houses.

You have to know what the house will sell for once it is fixed up. Otherwise, the cost of repairs, carrying costs, and what you buy it for mean nothing. You can ask a real estate agent what they think a house will be worth, but you should know as well to make sure the agent's numbers seem legit.

Determining market value isn't easy. You must look at a lot of houses, a lot of sold houses, and run a lot of numbers. If you cannot accurately figure out what a house will be worth, you are asking for trouble.

I would never rely on Zillow's value either. They can be right on or they can be 20 percent off. The tricky part knowing if Zillow is right or not. It takes work, but you have to know values and figure out what houses will be worth yourself. You can get help from agents, other investors, lenders, etc., but you need to learn to do it on your own and not rely on others.

7

High-End Houses Are Cool but Expensive to Flip! Be Very Careful

I flipped a high-end house around a year ago. It was a very risky flip because of the price point and the situation. A tenant with a 10-year lease in place lived there, and I needed to get rid of her.

I bought the house for $535,000 and sold it for $802,000. That was a huge spread, but we only made a little over $100,000 on the deal. (I say "only" as it relates to the $270,000 spread: I will take a $100,000 profit any day!). All the costs are higher with expensive homes, including the carrying costs, the taxes, the commissions, the financing costs, and the repairs.

Most people expect a high-end home to be perfect. You cannot get away with a decent rehab. It needs to be perfect. Even with a perfect rehab, selling a high-end home can be tough. They typically take longer to sell, and if the market is stagnant or falling, they can be much tougher to sell than lower-priced homes.

Some flippers make a lot of money flipping high-end homes, but you must be very careful and have a ton of room in the deal. I find it tough to find those deals in my market.

8

Television Shows Will Not Help You Learn to Flip Houses

HGTV can be very entertaining, but that is what their house flips shows are: entertainment. They are not real, and they do not portray real life. It takes me about five minutes of watching a house flipping show before I get frustrated.

House flipping shows often leave out many of the costs involved in flipping. They do not account for financing costs, carrying costs, and sometimes even selling costs. House flipping shows also show the hosts doing work all the time! That is not a smart way to run a flipping business.

I talked to one of the hosts about their show a few years ago. They said the show made them put up the tile in the bathroom shower. That was the first time the host had ever laid tile in a shower. His crew tore it out immediately after he did it and redid the entire thing.

House flipping shows also do not show some of the most important parts of flipping, like finding the deal and finding the money to buy and fix up that deal!

9

Great Contractors Are the Key to a Profitable Flipping Business

You cannot do all the work on a house flip yourself. You might be able to do it a few times, but you will get burned out eventually. You are also not creating a business if you must do all the work in it. You have to find great contractors and sub contractors.

Finding great contractors is not easy! It is one of the toughest parts of the business. We go through a rigorous process to find contractors, and many of them still do not work out. We find contractors through many sources: Craigslist, Facebook, Angieslist, Thumbtack, networking, and more.

When we find a contractor, we do not simply let them bid a job. We give them specific instructions on how to answer and apply for our job. If they do that right, we will meet them for lunch or at our office. We pay attention to timeliness and how prepared they are.

If the meeting goes well with them, we will meet them at a house. We will always start with small jobs for them to bid on. We always get a detailed bid before allowing any work to start. If the bid comes in at a decent price, we will try them out.

We visit the site often to make sure they are working and on schedule. We are very honest with what we want and with how they are doing throughout the process.

10

Don't Ever Open a Freezer or Fridge at House You Just Bought

I like to throw in some fun tips as well. One of the things I have learned on a couple of occasions is to never open a freezer at a house we just bought, especially if it is a stand-alone freezer. You never know what is in that freezer or how long it has been in there.

The last time I opened a freezer, it was full of deer meat that had been in the freezer for months, and the freezer was off. I quickly closed it, but will never forget that smell.

We told our contractors not to open it and throw it straight in the dumpster. They managed to drop it while trying to get it into the dumpster. I hear it was not a pretty site, but luckily I was not there!

11

There Is No Need to Spend $40,000 on a House Flipping Course to Be Successful

A dvertisements for house-flipping seminars are all over the radio, Facebook, and many other social media sites. The seminars advertise famous flippers as the teachers. There are a lot of problems with these seminars.

The famous person they use to draw people in will not be there. They do not teach the courses. Their name is used to get people in the door.

Once you are in the door, you will learn very little. The seminar is meant to be very motivating and get you pumped up. However, it is not meant to teach you any of the details. You have to go to the boot camp for the real coaching.

At the boot camp, you get pumped up again, but you won't gain much in the way of actual learning. Instead, you find out you need to spend tens of thousands of dollars to get the real coaching. They make it sound like success is impossible without this coaching but virtually guaranteed with it.

You will probably learn more from this book than you will from the $40,000 in coaching you get. The part that makes me mad is they encourage people to

THERE IS NO NEED TO SPEND $40,000 ON A HOUSE FLIPPING COURSE...

get credit cards, borrow money, or take out loans to pay for the coaching.

12

Time is Money! It Can Cost From $50 to $100 a Day to Own a Moderately Priced Flip

Many people do not realize how much money it takes to flip a house. The costs add up very quickly. Aside from the repairs, carrying costs and financing costs will also add to the cost. Depending on the price of the home, the type of financing, and many other factors, it can easily cost $50, $100, or more a day to own a flip.

I finance all of my flips because I make more money in the long run using loans. A $200,000 loan can cost from $27 to $65 a day in interest alone depending on the type of financing being used.

Utilities can run $10 a day depending on the house.

Property taxes can be from $5 to $30 a day depending on the state you are in.

Insurance can be $5 a day.

Maintenance may also be needed, or there may be HOA or other costs while

TIME IS MONEY! IT CAN COST FROM $50 TO $100 A DAY TO OWN A...

you own a flip. This is why it is so important to flip houses quickly and not underestimate the costs.

13

There Will Be Rough Times. You Cannot Give Up

No matter what you do in life, there will be good times and bad times. True character is shown in the bad times, not the good times. House flipping is no different. In fact, there may be a lot more bad times than good times when you first start!

So many things can go wrong when you flip houses. The repairs can take longer or cost more than you thought. There are almost always extra costs that come up that were not accounted for. You may not sell a house right away. Multiple contracts could fall apart. There could be appraisal issues, inspection issues, permit issues, etc. The list of things that could go wrong goes on and on.

It may seem crazy that people want to flip houses, but remember that you can make a lot of money from one deal. If you can flip multiple houses at the same time, it can be a very lucrative career. If you do things right, bad things will still happen, but the good will outweigh the bad by far.

You must be ready for the bad times. Don't let them get you down. Plow through them until you get back to the good times again.

14

Leave Your Emotions at the Door

Buying a house is a very emotional process for many people. Many flippers know that paint colors and other things that are super cheap to fix make a huge difference to home buyers. They let their emotions decide what house to buy whether they know it or not.

While we flip houses to play to home buyers' emotions, flippers need to be careful not to let their emotions get involved in their business. I have let my emotions play a part when deciding which house to buy. I restored a 1900s house because I thought it would be so neat to see the house fixed up. I knew I may not make a lot of money on the deal, and I did not.

I have also bid too high on homes at auctions because I let my emotions take over. I wanted to beat the person I was bidding against, even if it meant I was paying more than I said I would at the beginning of the auction.

I have also gotten angry at contractors, inspectors, buyers, agents, and lenders. As we already talked about, a lot can go wrong. While there are good reasons to be angry, anger usually does not solve anything (though, in some cases, getting angry at contractors has helped immensely).

Most of the time, it is best to keep your emotions in check. We think better when we are calm and using our heads...not our hearts.

15

Do Not Underestimate the Cost of a Trash-out or Eviction

Avoid Evictions

I buy many houses that are occupied by tenants or the previous owners or need a lot of trash removed. It is easy to overlook these costs and only think of the repairs that will be needed once the people are out and all the stuff is gone.

Removing junk can be very costly. It is a disgusting, time-consuming job and is not fun for the guys doing the job. Dumps and dumpsters are expensive as well. It can easily take a couple thousand of dollars just for a basic trash-out on a house. If a hoarder lives (or lived there), the cost can double.

Evictions can be very costly as well. We try to avoid evictions by offering cash for keys. We will pay the tenant or previous occupant a couple of thousand dollars to move out by a certain date. They only get paid once they are out, not before.

If an eviction is necessary, you need to take into account the time you are owning the property and paying all the costs we mentioned previously. The eviction itself can cost thousands of dollars, and hopefully, the tenants do not trash the property more!

We always hire an attorney to handle the eviction so we do not mess anything up! Buying occupied or trashed houses can be a great way to get deals, but be prepared to spend a lot more money on the rehab or evictions!

16

Always Get the HVAC Checked Out No Matter How New It Is

We have bought houses that were less than ten years old and had what seemed like a great furnace or air conditioner. We always have our HVAC systems checked out to make sure they are in clean and in good condition. Often, a newer furnace will be bad, spewing out dangerous levels of carbon monoxide.

A furnace should last up to 30 years, but that does not mean they always do. If a furnace is not cleaned or air filters are not changed, it drastically reduces the lifespan. We have seen many furnaces needing replacement that were less than 10 years old.

Always get your HVAC systems checked out no matter how new they look. The last thing I want to ever see happen in our homes is someone getting hurt or worse. We also always make sure we have carbon monoxide and smoke detectors in the homes.

17

Waiving the Inspection Is a Great Way to Get More Deals

I buy a lot of my house flips from the MLS (multiple listing service). Many people say getting deals from the MLS is impossible because there is too much competition. However, we are in one of the hottest markets in the country and still get deals from the MLS all the time. It is not easy, but it is possible.

One reason I am able to get so many deals from the MLS is I waive my inspection on almost every house I offer on. I have gotten deals where other people offered $10,000 more than I did because I waived my inspection and had no loan conditions.

Waiving your inspection does not work on every offer, but it does on some. It also helps that I am an agent/broker and can act very quickly when I see a deal pop up.

I would not advise that new investors waive their inspection as it can get you into trouble. You need to be very confident in your ability to judge the repairs on a house and leave room for any unforeseen repairs that may pop up. I can usually tell what a house needs in a 10 minute walk through.

18

Home Depot and Lowes Have Great Programs for Flippers

I used to shop around all over to get materials for my flips. Or, I let my contractors decide when and where to buy materials. In the last two years, I have bought almost everything from Home Depot. They have great prices and great programs for flippers.

We have a managed pro account which means we get very special treatment. You have to spend about $125,000 a year to qualify. We get the pro desk discounts, discounts in the bid room, and .5 % cash back.

We also get 2 percent cash back by being part of a local real estate investor meetup. I use my credit card to buy almost everything at Home Depot which is another 2 percent cash back.

We also get dibs on many clearance items and a lot of personal help with many different items. Lowes for Pros has a similar, but in my opinion, lesser program.

By controlling everything our contractors buy, we also save money. Many of our contractors would go to other stores that are much more expensive because it was easier.

19

While Neutral Colors Sell, You Do Not Have to Be Boring

Neutral colors sell houses. You want to appeal to the most people you can, and neutral almost always accomplishes that. However, you do not have to be boring when picking paint or other fixtures.

I know a lot of flippers who use the same materials, paint colors, flooring, and fixtures on every single house. We sell a lot of houses, and it is fun for us to try out new design options. Different houses also look better with different paint colors or designs.

Nikki, my project manager, likes to surprise me once in a while and try new designs out without telling me. They are not crazy paint colors or super trendy ideas. They're subtle changes. It is a great way to try things out and hone in on what our favorites are.

Have fun when flipping! While you should try to leave your emotions out of the business decisions, that does not mean you cannot be creative.

20

Selling a House in the Winter Is Not Always Bad

Many people want to sell a house until the spring. They think there are no buyers in the winter, and they will lose a ton of money selling then. True, some houses sell for less in the winter, but some houses also sell for less in the summer.

I have been an investor and agent for more than 17 years, and some winters are great for selling a house and some are bad. Buyers are always looking to buy houses, and sometimes, they look in the winter. While spring might have more buyers looking than winter, spring will also have many more houses for sale. Think of all the other sellers who are waiting for spring to come so they can list their house.

As a house flipper, I never wait more than a few days to list my finished product. We may wait to list until after the weekend or after a holiday, but we do not wait weeks or months. We want to keep the money moving and get it into the next deal as quickly as we can.

21

Being Too Trendy Can Make It Tougher to Sell a Flip

When flipping houses, you want to keep up with the times, but you do not want to be *too* trendy. You want to appeal to the most people you can without being on the fringes of outdated or too new. One way to figure out the best design choices is to look at newly constructed homes. Look at the big builders and see what they are doing. They want to appeal to as many people as possible and will base their designs on what sells best.

For us, we do not like oak cabinets, but we aren't going crazy with bright blue cabinets either. We don't mind using grays or other colors that have become more mainstream now. We stayed away from too many grays when it first became trendy because most people were not on board yet.

We also do not make every house the same. We like to use different colors and designs to keep things interesting. But what works for you may not work for us and vice versa. If you happen to be flipping in a super trendy area and all your comps are using brand-new design trends, you may have to go that route. However, I think there are very few places where that is necessary, and keeping ahead of the curve usually costs a lot of money.

22

Check Your Properties at Least Once a Week

One of the fastest ways for a house flipper to find themselves in heaps of trouble is to ignore their properties or contractors. I have been guilty of this on many occasions, and it almost never works out well no matter how good the contractor is or how many times you have used them.

In one situation, a contractor told us he was almost done with a flip. We were really dumb and did not check on the home for over a month. It was about 30 minutes from us, and we had a lot of other things going on (which is no excuse). When we visited the house, the work had not even started! The contractor claimed his guys had lied to him about the work being done, but it was obvious he had not been there either...or he was flat out lying to us.

We fired that contract and never used him again. I have had other problems with contractors not working when they know I am not checking on them as often as I should be. It is natural for people to get away with what they can get away with no matter how good of a person they are.

I check my houses at least once every two weeks but prefer to check them at least every week, if not more often. The more I check them, the faster my guys work, and the more they are on their toes. I also do not tell them when I am coming. One contractor always called me and told me when to come see the house. He made sure his entire crew was there. If I showed up uninvited, there was maybe one guy working, if anyone. I wondered why it was taking a crew of five guys so long to finish a remodel!

23

Making a House Perfect Is Not Possible

I know many people who are perfectionists. Being perfect is a great trait for some jobs or businesses, but not for house flipping. There is too much work to do on a house, and you will always find something else that needs to be done. Look at new builds. They are not close to perfect, and they are starting from scratch with everything new.

We do not cut corners on safety issues like HVAC, electrical, plumbing, etc. We make sure the house is solid and will be a good home, but we don't have to fix everything for it to sell. On some houses, we do not do anything to the yards, which drives some people crazy. However, we do not have to make the yards perfect for them to sell because many home buyers feel they can do that work themselves.

If we can save money on painting cabinets instead of buying new ones, we will. If we can avoid removing walls or changing the floor plan, we will. I love cosmetic flips because less can go wrong. The more you try to fix, the longer it will take, and the more problems you will have.

It will take almost as long to make the last last 10 percent of a flip perfect as it will to complete the first 90 percent, and 90 percent of people will not know the difference.

24

The Older a Home Is, the More Problems it Can Have

I have flipped both newer and older houses and made decent money on both. I wish all my flips were newer because it would make life so much easier. The electric, HVAC, plumbing, and foundations are all so much better on most new houses. Newer houses also have egress windows in the basements, yet many older houses do not.

While I can make money on older houses, I prefer to flip newer houses. The problem is there are not always newer houses available to flip! I can also make decent money on older houses. I am very careful when flipping older houses and pay close attention to the condition they are in. Old houses can easily break the bank with a few unforeseen repairs. It can cost $10,000 or more to replace an electrical system or foundation.

I am not saying you should not flip older houses, but you must be very careful and assume you will run into known problems. If you are dealing with a major rehab on an older house, make sure there is a ton of room for profit and things that could go wrong. Some of my biggest headaches have come from older houses that appeared to have huge profit margins, but the endless repairs ate up that margin quickly.

25

Do Not Work on the Houses Yourself

Many house flippers work on the houses themselves to save money. I did this once in 2006 because I thought it would be a great way to get ahead. I would do all the manual labor myself and make twice as much money because I would not have to pay a contractor.

I wish the story had ended up that way, but it did not. I did most of the work myself, including paint, flooring, kitchen, baths, windows, doors, lights, and more. I saved some money on labor because I was doing the work, but I had my worst year ever in the real estate business.

The problem was that I was focused on making an hourly wage. I was doing all this work on the house and ignoring all of my other work. I was not selling houses as an agent or looking for new houses to flip. That was not the only problem.

I had no clue what I was doing. I had some construction experience, but I was not qualified to be doing all the work I was doing. It took me three times as long as it would have taken a professional, and the work was not nearly as good. I had to have some contractors come in and fix the stuff I messed up or did not know how to do.

I was also miserable. It takes so much longer than you think it will to fix up a house. It is not something you can do a few nights a week and on the weekends. You need to be there full time, and if you are there full time, when do you have time to manage the business?

You may be able to flip a house or two a year doing the work yourself, but if you want to scale and create a business, you will need to figure out a way to get the houses repaired without you doing the work.

26

Do Not Discount the MLS Even in a Hot Market

Many people made a lot of money flipping houses from the MLS after the housing crash. Foreclosures were all over the place, and buying from banks, making some quick repairs, and selling for a profit seemed easy. Foreclosures have since dissipated in many parts of the country, and buying from banks is not as easy as it used to be. Because of the difficulty finding foreclosures, many people have proclaimed that getting a deal from the MLS is impossible.

MLS stands for multiple listing service and is where real estate agents or brokers list houses for sale. Many people assume you can only get deals on foreclosures from the MLS, but I buy most of my flips from the MLS, and they are very rarely foreclosures. You can get many types of deals on the MLS, and you should not be ignoring it.

When someone tells me there are no deals on the MLS, I usually ask a few questions. How are you looking? Are you an agent? How often do you check new listings? I usually find out pretty quickly that the person is not really looking for deals on the MLS. In fact, most people admit there are deals on the MLS. They are just not the ones who are getting those deals. They say properties go too quickly, and they don't have a chance to see them, or other investors always beat them out.

Finding deals isn't easy. Otherwise, everyone would be buying real estate like crazy. No matter where you look for deals, it is not easy. If you want to find deals from the MLS, it will take hard work and patience. I am a real estate agent, which gives me a huge advantage in finding deals and saving money on commissions. I search for deals multiple times a day and act very quickly if one comes up. I might go weeks without seeing a great deal, but I do not give up because I know they will eventually show up.

27

Never Trust a Wholesaler's Numbers. Verify Everything.

Wholesalers can be another great source of deals. I buy houses from wholesalers all the time. However, a lot of people call themselves wholesalers yet do not know what they are doing. It takes sifting through a lot of wannabees before you find a good wholesaler who has deals.

When you find a wholesaler who has deals, you cannot blindly trust what they tell you. You need to know your market, what the values are, and what the repairs will cost. If you are relying on a wholesaler, real estate agent, or anyone to tell you what to do, you will be in trouble.

Many wholesalers leave out all the costs that come with flipping, including carrying, selling, and financing costs. They also may exaggerate the ARV or underestimate the repairs. I never trust the numbers anyone gives me. I verify everything and come up with my own number for what will make the deal work.

Here is what a wholesaler might advertise:
  -Purchase price: $100,000
  -ARV: $150,000

NEVER TRUST A WHOLESALER'S NUMBERS. VERIFY EVERYTHING.

-Repairs needed: $25,000
-Profit: $25,000!

That sounds great, except they left out the selling costs ($10,000), the financing costs, the carrying costs, and the buying costs. This deal would actually lose money after all those costs are considered.

28

Make Sure You Are Following All EPA Guidelines

When you repair houses, you might use a licensed contractor who follows all guidelines, has all the needed certifications, and knows the laws. You also might hire a handyman who simply wants to make a few bucks and couldn't care less what the laws say.

The Environmental Protection Agency sets strict guidelines on how to do certain things, like removing lead-based paint. Houses that were built before 1978 may have lead-based paint, which can be very dangerous to children. If the paint is on the walls, it usually does not harm anyone, but if it is disturbed or chipping, it can be very dangerous.

Certain guidelines exist for how to remove lead-based paint. Contractors who are removing the paint should be certified to remove it and follow those guidelines. If your contractors are not following the guidelines, they could be fined tens of thousands of dollars, or you could be fined if you are telling those contractors what to do.

29

Some Houses Are Not Worth Flipping No Matter What the Price

Some properties seem so cheap that they would have to make a great flip even though they have major problems. I have bought some of these houses, and they never seem to turn out like I think they will. Some problems and properties are just not worth dealing with.

Some houses are tiny—I mean 200-square-feet tiny—and are almost impossible to sell. Houses with only one bedroom are very tough to sell. Some houses that are right on a busy street can be a nightmare to sell. No matter what the price is, you are better off not buying some houses. Even if you can make a little money off them, the hassle and pain is just not worth it.

Houses are cheap for a number of reasons, and one of those reasons is very few people will ever want to buy them no matter what you do. Be careful with those houses!

Here are some things to watch out for:
 -Houses on very busy streets
 -Houses that are tiny compared to other houses in the area
 -Houses that are huge compared to other houses in the area

- Houses with access problems
- Houses in flood zone
- Houses that need major structural work
- Houses that have been contaminated with meth or mold
- Houses in extremely rural areas

30

Busy Roads Can Make a House a Nightmare to Sell

We have sold a number of houses on busy roads, and I always try to account for the discount the property will need to be sold at because of the busy road. However, I never seem to account for enough of a discount or the extra time it takes to sell a house on a busy road.

If a house is on a two-lane road that is somewhat more busy than a neighborhood road, the price might not be affected very much. The issue we have is trying sell houses that are on four-lane roads with a lot of traffic.

People with families simply do not want to live on busy roads due to safety concerns for their children. No matter how cheap the house is, they will not want it. The roads also are very noisy and give people a bad feeling about the homes no matter how nice they are.

I feel at least a 20 percent discount is needed to sell homes on busy roads, and it usually takes 2 to 3 times longer to sell those homes. Every time we buy a house on a busy road, it comes back to bite us. A house on a busy road now has to be an incredible deal for us to consider buying it.

31

Buying a House Occupied by Tenants Can be a Great Way to Get a Good Deal

One way to get a great deal is to take on houses occupied by tenants. Many landlords end up with problem tenants, or they want to sell right away but have a long-term lease in place. They try to sell even though tenants live in the house, but that eliminates most buyers who want to move into the property right away.

Occupied houses can be a great good deal but can be risky. You never know what kind of tenant you are inheriting or what it will take to get them out. If you buy a house with a long-term lease in place, you cannot just kick out the tenants because you are the new owners: you must take over the lease as well.

If the lease goes for another year and the tenants want to stay, as long as they keep paying and do not break any rules, you cannot kick them out early. I once bought a flip that had a ten-year lease in place. We think the lease was bogus, but the courts upheld it, even after the home went through foreclosure. We got an amazing deal on the home, and were able to negotiate a cash-for-keys arrangement with the tenants.

Cash for keys is a great way to get tenants out, even if their lease is expiring.

We offer the tenants a certain amount of money to break their lease and move out early. Or, we even offer a bonus if they move out on time and leave the place in good shape. Cash for keys usually works well because the tenants know they will need to be moving soon anyway, and they might as well make some extra money.

We have offered $500 or $20,000 for cash for keys depending on the situation and what it was worth to us. The tenants do not have to accept the cash-for-keys agreement, and you must be prepared to wait them out if they want to stay.

32

Prep the Listing Agent before Sending in a Low Offer

I get a lot of deals from the MLS. Sometimes, I offer above list price, and sometimes I send in low offers. I do not send low offers in often, but when I do, I prep the listing agent. Letting the listing agent know a low offer is coming in works much better.

I have been an agent and broker for many years. I have gotten great offers and very low offers. When an offer comes in without any warning, I usually assume it is a decent offer, as most offers are close to listing price. You get excited that you received an offer for your clients.

When you open up that offer and see a low price, it is deflating. All that work, finally an offer comes in, and it is super low. Now you have to tell your clients you received an offer, but it is not quite what they were hoping for.

Before I send a low offer in, I will contact the listing agent. In some cases, I will email the agent and tell them I might bring a low offer, but there will be no inspection and a quick closing. Would their seller consider a lower offer? Most of the time the agent will encourage us to send the offer, even though it will be low.

PREP THE LISTING AGENT BEFORE SENDING IN A LOW OFFER

By preparing the listing agent for a low offer, we set the right state of mind. They are ready for that low offer and are not expecting a good offer that will disappoint them when they see the price. If the listing agent is disappointed, they will convey that to their clients, even if they are not trying to. If they are not disappointed, you have a much better chance of your offer being accepted.

33

Always Check for Flood Zones before Buying a House

Flood zones can greatly affect the value of a property. The insurance is higher, and many buyers obviously worry about their home being in a flood zone. In certain flood areas, you cannot get insurance at all on homes, and you are not even allowed to rebuild the home if the property is more than 50 percent damaged.

The tricky part about flood zones is they can change. FEMA controls where the flood zones are, and those zones change with new storms or new river paths. If you bought a home that was not in a flood zone 10 years ago, that does not mean it is not in one now. You also cannot use common sense to know what a flood zone is and what is not.

Some houses will be right next to rivers or the ocean where you have a pretty good idea that they are in a flood zone. Other properties will be surrounded by dry land, but there may be a dry creek bed you cannot even see that causes the property to be in a flood zone. Some properties may be next to rivers yet elevated 30 feet and still in the flood zone, or maybe they aren't.

If you are getting a loan, the lender will almost always order a flood certificate

ALWAYS CHECK FOR FLOOD ZONES BEFORE BUYING A HOUSE

to make sure the property is not in a flood zone. However, if you are paying cash or using private money, you may not know the property is in a flood zone until you try to sell it again! FEMA has flood maps that show where the zones are, and checking properties before you buy them is wise!

34

Make Sure All Broken Windows and Doors Are Boarded or Fixed

When you buy houses that you intend to flip, they are not always in great shape. Even though you buy them in rough condition, it doesn't mean you are off the hook as far as safety goes. If there are broken windows or broken doors, you need to fix them asap.

The last think I ever want to see are some kids messing around one of my houses and getting hurt. Abandoned or dilapidated houses are a magnet for curious people. If you have a property that looks really run down with broken windows and doors, people will want to go inside and check it out. After all, look at the place! Who will care?!

If someone gets in the house and gets hurt, you could be held liable. We board up all broken windows as soon as we buy the property and plan to replace them shortly thereafter. A boarded up houses attracts unwanted attention as well. If the door won't lock or someone has broken into a house, fix it ASAP.

If squatters move in, they may try to claim they are occupants and you have to evict them to make them leave. Make sure the house is secure and safe, and try not to leave vacant properties sitting around for years.

35

Beware of the Fake Private-Money Lender!

P rivate money is one of the best things for flippers: a lender who is easy to work with, has plenty of money, and is looking for the right flipper. The truth is that private money usually comes from someone you know, not people posting on Facebook real estate groups.

I run a real estate group, and I receive multiple emails from scamming private-money lenders each week. They advertise how awesome they are, how much money they have to lend, and how cheap it is. They usually say the rates are 5 percent (private money almost never is that cheap), they can loan up to 50 million dollars (run away), and can fund right away with no credit check. If it sounds too good to be true, it probably is!

These lenders are not really looking to give you any money: they want your money. They will ask for an application fee, and as soon as you send it, you will never hear from them again. If someone offers you a deal that sounds too good to be true, it probably is. Random people on Facebook are not going to be the ones to lend you money.

36

The 90-Day Flip Rule Can Make it Tough to Sell Fast

We all have the goal of flipping houses fast, or at least we should! The faster you can flip a house, the more money you will make because you decrease carrying and financing costs. Nothing sucks more than finally getting that quick flip under contract and then realizing you must wait for the 90-day flip rule.

FHA loans have a rule that says a house cannot be "flipped" within 90 days. That means if you buy a house, fix it up, and try to sell it again to an FHA buyer within 90 days, the deal most likely will not go through. The rule does not say you have to wait 90 days to sell the property but that you must wait 90 days to write the contract!

This rule originated with FHA, but that does not mean only FHA loans use it. Many conventional lenders adopt the same rules as FHA and will have the rule as well.

Another FHA rule states that if the house sells for more than 100 percent of the last purchase price within 180 days, there needs to be a second appraisal to confirm value. Be prepared for that one as well!

37

Flips Are More of a Job Than an Investment

While I love flipping houses, it is not a passive-income business for the most part. We have to constantly find and buy new houses in order to make money. It can be set up as a business, which we have done, with staff, employees, and a lot of help. Flipping is still a job or a business, not an investment in the sense that money will keep coming without working.

Rentals are more of a true investment because you can buy them and have a property manager do almost all of the work. They become a passive investment that brings money in every month whether you work or not. I like to use the money I make from flipping or being an agent to buy as many rentals as I can.

I love flipping, but I love the passive income that comes with rentals as well.

38

Remember to Take Time off and Enjoy What Your Hard Work Created

House flipping is a time-consuming business, especially if you do not follow all of the tips in this book and do the work yourself on houses. Even if you hire out the work, there is a lot to do. It is easy to get bogged down and forget to take time off.

Some of my best ideas come while on vacation and not thinking about work. Vacations give our brains time to relax, to clear, and to look at things in a different way. We can often do many extremely simple things to improve our business. If we are always working, it is really hard to see those things. However, if we take some time off and step away from the day-to-day activities, we often get those "ah ha" moments. We see things that can get us more deals, better financing, work faster, or ways to delegate more and free up our own time.

Do not be afraid to take time off. Do not be afraid to hire help so that you can take more time off as well!

39

You Do Not Have to Buy a Foreclosure to Get a Good Deal

Many new flippers think they have to buy foreclosures to get a good deal. Now that there are far fewer foreclosures than there have been in the past, people think flipping homes is impossible. That could not be further from the truth. In the past, foreclosures were a great source of deals. As a house flipper, you should have many sources of deals, not just one!

I have flipped more than 50 houses in the last two years, and I think 2 of those were foreclosures of some kind. There are almost no foreclosures in my market, yet we keep getting deals. There are so many ways to get deals, and buying foreclosures is not at the top of the list.

We buy from the MLS, wholesalers, FSBOs, and we do our own direct marketing. Never narrow your search to one type of deal!

40

Pre-Inspecting a Home Can Help with the Scope of Work for the Contractor

When I buy houses, I almost never get an inspection. I am also very experienced and know what to look for in a house. For a while, we would have inspections done on our homes right after we bought them. This would give us an idea of what work needed to be done.

We stopped doing that because we almost always send in our electricians, plumbers, HVAC guys, and more to check everything out anyway. We found doing an inspection was slowing us down, and our subs usually know more than inspectors.

That does not mean having inspections done is not useful for other flippers. I think it can be a great way to know what is needed, repair wise, on a home. It can also be a great way to see how your contractors or subs evaluate a home if you are using them for the first time. You can compare what they found to what the inspector found.

41

You Don't Get to Keep Everything in a House When You Buy it; Check Local Laws

We once found a late-model BMW in the garage of a house we bought at the foreclosure sale. Some people thought, "Wow! You got a car!" Nope. For one, you cannot simply keep a car just because you found it or someone left it on your property. Removing cars can be a pain even if they are abandoned.

Secondly, there are laws and rules about what you must do with things left in houses. If valuables are left in a house, you do not get to just keep them. You may have to hold them in storage for a certain amount of time or go through a personal property eviction. In Colorado, if the garage-sale value of the items left in a house is more than $300, you must complete a personal property eviction with the county sheriff. This process can take a month, but that is what the law states.

If you can get the previous owners or occupants to sign off that they do not want any of the things they left in the house, you may be able to avoid the personal property eviction. Make sure you know what the laws are in your state before you go keeping everything you find in homes.

42

Ask the Title Company For a Hold Open Policy to Save Money

Title insurance is one of the more expensive selling or buying costs if the buyer must pay it. It can cost thousands of dollars depending on the state and how it is handled. Again, title insurance is different everywhere and basically guarantees clear title to the new owners of the home with some exceptions. Typically the seller pays for title insurance, but in some cases, the buyer might have to pay on auction, wholesaler, or HUD deals.

When flipping houses, you can get what is called a hold open policy. You are buying and selling the house in a short period of time. The title company has a much easier job insuring the home when you sell it because you just bought it and they already issued clear title. Most title companies offer this policy, which allows the flipper to buy and sell the home at the same title company but pay a much lower price for the title insurance the second time around.

43

Right Now is the Perfect Time of Year to Sell

Many people ask if waiting to sell their flip is smart. Maybe it is the dead of winter and spring is a better time to sell in your market. I, personally, do not wait to sell my flips unless there is a major holiday coming up, and in that case, I only wait a few days to list the home.

If you wait months to sell your house, the holding costs will most likely eat up any gain you have from selling for a higher price. You are also risking prices dropping with a market correction the longer you hold onto a property.

The biggest reason I do not wait to sell is I want to keep my money moving. I want to be in and out of properties as quickly as possible because that is where the money is made. Trying to eek out a few thousand dollars may cost me much more money because I missed a deal since my money was tied up.

44

Beware of Structural Problems

I mention this often, but the bigger a rehab is, the more problems you can run into. We have done many big rehabs on houses with structural issues. The properties usually have big profit potential that quickly decreases as the deal progresses. The problem with big rehabs is that so many things can go wrong. They almost always do go wrong! Completing big rehabs also takes a lot of resources. My guys could be working on other properties that will make close to as much money and take half the time if they were not stuck on these big jobs.

The biggest rehabs seem to come with structural problems. I have redone entire foundations before, and it is not pretty. Not only are you paying $15,000 or more in some cases to redo the foundation, but you are also moving the house around. Everything cracks and breaks, even the things you were hoping to keep. A new foundation can easily add $30,000 to the rehab budget even if you have an amazingly cheap foundation person. It is easy to pay much much more.

You also need to pay and schedule a structural engineer, which can costs thousands of dollars and add weeks or months to the schedule. You need to have permits in most places with massive repairs like this, which can add even more money.

BEWARE OF STRUCTURAL PROBLEMS

The more you open up a house, the more you find that needs fixed. Once all the walls are open, you may see there is no insulation, the wiring is all bad, or the vents are wrong. Now there is rotten wood that needs to be replaced. Not only does all of this take more money, it also takes more time. The longer it takes, the more carrying costs you have, and the longer your guys are tied up.

I am at a point now where I try to avoid all huge rehabs, especially if they have structural problems.

45

Simple Touches Can Add a Lot of Value

While we try not to overdo our rehabs, we do not make them look plain. We try to add cheap and effective design features that will jazz up a house. We might paint the front door a different color, add shutters, put in decent-looking light fixtures, update appliances, etc.

You do not have to go to a designer store to pick decent-looking fixtures either. You can pick things at Home Depot that will be affordable and make the home look nice. Simple things can make a home look great without breaking the bank.

46

Restoring is Different than Renovating

I restored a house that was built in the 1920s. It was a beautiful house with original trim, floors, doors, and more. We could have painted the trim, replaced the doors, and made it look modern, but we chose to restore it.

Restoring a house is much more tedious and expensive than renovating a house. Making the old work with the new is not easy. I did not make very much money on this house, and I knew that I wouldn't going into the deal. I knew that it was a labor of love and not a smart business decision.

The house turned out great, and we sold it, but I would never do it again. It was a massive undertaking, and we had a very limited market to sell it to. Many people say they love old original houses, but they don't actually want to live in them. They want to visit them and then go live in their comfy house with all the modern designs and amenities.

Be very careful taking when on restorations!

47

Small Houses May Not Sell for as Much, But They Are Much Cheaper to Fix

I love working on small houses because they are so much cheaper and easier to fix than expensive houses. Even a simple cosmetic remodel on a big house can be very expensive. You have more paint, more flooring, a larger roof, bigger kitchens, more baths, and a larger heating system.

The bigger a house is, the more can go wrong. If you end up finding a problem with the electrical, the plumbing, or something else, fixing it is much more expensive. If you have to tear into walls, everything becomes more expensive!

It may seem neat to take on big houses, but you must account for the extra costs that will come with larger houses.

48

Don't Ever Assume Prices Will Go Up, Leading to a Profit

We have seen some crazy price appreciation in many markets. That price appreciation has hidden many mistakes flippers make. Hold on to a property for 14 months, and the price increase makes all the extra costs seem okay. This has happened on my deals quite a bit. I make big mistakes and get bailed out by increasing prices. I did not plan for prices to increase, but it sure was nice!

Some investors will take it further and buy flips hoping that prices will increase, resulting in a profit. This is a very risky strategy as no one knows what the market will do. This happened before the last housing crisis and bankrupted many investors who were not even trying to get a good deal but were hoping for price increases.

I always invest thinking prices could decrease...not increase. This gives me an added layer of protection to keep my profit margins high in case we see a market downturn.

49

Unique Homes Are Interesting but Often Hard to Sell

I love cool and unique houses. However, uniqueness does not mean they are a good investment. The problem with unique houses is they are very hard to value. If they are hard to value, it is easy to overestimate their value and lose money.

Unique houses can also be very hard to sell because they may only appeal to a very small portion of the market. They can increase the marketing time and costs on the flip. Remember that just because you think it is a cool house does not mean everyone thinks it is a cool house.

Finally, unique houses can be hard for an appraiser to value. Even if you find the perfect buyer who is willing to pay for the cool factor, the appraiser will have limited comps and may come in well below contract value.

50

Design Choices Can be Region Specific; Study Your Market

If you live on the coast, people will expect different design choices than if you live in the mountains. People ask me why I don't tile entire houses: it's because most people don't like cold tile everywhere, especially in a climate like Colorado's. But tile in a house next to the beach makes sense. Landscaping, paint, flooring, all can change based on your location. Study you market and see what is popular.

Many people ask me why all my houses have textured walls. That is very common in Colorado. Almost every house has it. In other areas, it is not common at all. Different areas have different trends for colors, kitchens, baths, flooring, landscaping, fencing, garages, heating, air conditioning, and more. Even different neighborhoods in the same town can have different design trends.

Do not assume that what you see on TV is what you should do to your houses. Research your market and the houses you will be competing against to see what does or does not need to be done.

51

Laminate Flooring Is One Way to Save Money

We try to save hardwood and refinish it. However, we rarely, if ever, install hardwood. It can be very expensive, and on the houses we remodel, it does not add as much value as the extra cost.

If we are starting from scratch, we almost always use laminate or a vinyl plank. Most buyers have accepted that not every house will have real hardwood and are okay with the much-cheaper substitute.

If a house has a lot of hardwood already and there are just a few areas where it is missing, we might add hardwood if it can be matched. We can source the hardwood from Home Depot, but we let our hardwood guys do the matching and decide the best route to take.

Some hardwood is too far gone to be saved, and we leave that up to our hardwood guys to decide. Hardwood is nice, but it is not necessary.

52

Never Pay Contractors in Full until the Job Is Done

One of my worst contractor experiences came when my bookkeeper paid a contractor a 2nd time on a bill I already paid. I forgot to mark "paid" on the bill. That was the contractor's final payment, and he stopped working almost immediately. It took 6 months to get him to finish the work. I've had other issues where I paid contractors when they said they were done but were not.

Make sure everything is done before you issue final payment. Nothing is more frustrating than waiting 3 weeks for final touch-up items to be done because the contractor already got paid and is in no rush. Many will claim they are almost done and promise to finish up but need the money right away. That is fine. Just promise to pay them as soon as those final items are done!

53

Try Not to Pay a Contractor Too Much Money Upfront

I know so many people who have been burned by paying too much money up front. I know contractors who have bid super low on multiple jobs at once to get multiple deposits on work and skipped town. A contractor can place a lien on a house fairly easily if they don't get paid. We have to sue them to get our money back. If a contractor says they need money for materials, buy the materials yourself. Then, they can't mark them up either. There is no reason a contractor needs 50 percent or more up front.

We pay 25 percent to start, 25 percent at the halfway point, and the final 50 percent when everything is done. A huge red flag is when a contractor demands a ton of money up front and will not work unless they are paid that money. In the past, we have had contractors we never paid a dime until all the work was done. That is tough to find now, but make sure you are not paying too much before any work is started.

54

No Matter How it Looks in the Movie, Don't Slide Down a Trash Chute

I think it is hilarious when people in movies jump into dumpsters thinking it will be soft and fun. My dumpsters are full of some dangerous stuff that I would not want to fall in from 6 inches, let alone 3 stories.

This a reminder to be careful on the worksite. There are a lot of dangerous things like nails, glass, uneven floors, holes and more. Make sure the job site is as safe as it can be, and be careful when overseeing the work!

55

The More Subcontractors You Can Find the Better

We use as many subcontractors as we can. We have subs for painting, electric, plumbing, HVAC, roofs, flooring, and much more. I find that using subs gets a job done faster and cheaper. However, scheduling everyone takes more management and time. Luckily, I have a project manager that handles all of that.

A GC (General Contractor) is nice because they oversee the entire project, but they are expensive. I prefer to use many subs and have my project manager or myself act as the GC. I have worked with many GCs who tried to have their own guys do all the work, and it takes forever. In my experience, it is better to have subs or specialists do the work. We hire out electricians, plumbers, roofers, drywall, foundation, painting, landscaping, HVAC, and more. It takes work, but we can get things done cheaper and better when hiring out as many subs as we can.

56

Be Careful Not to Get Caught Up in Bidding Wars

I have bid too highly on houses, wanting to "beat" the other bidder. It usually does not work out well. Stick to your number and you will be much better off, even if you don't get the property.

When bidding on or buying real estate, you need to leave your emotions out of it. It is easy to want to beat the other guy or think that they are willing to pay that much for a property, so I should be willing to pay that much as well! The other person may be thinking the exact same thing, and now both of you are paying much more than you should. Stick to your number and let the other person overpay.

57

Too Many Low-Ball Offers Can Be a Bad Thing

I may send in a low-ball offer once in a while, but I am very careful about it. I want to protect my reputation so that other agents take me seriously. I also may offer more than list price to get a deal. It all depends on the house and the circumstances.

I see some agents send in a low-ball offer on every property that is distressed or may be a decent deal. They are hoping that one out of a 100 sellers will take their crazy offer, but all they are doing is ruining their reputation. Agents will not take them seriously and may not present their offer, even if they are legally obligated to.

Be calculating when submitting low offers. Look for properties that show signs the seller is motivated.

58

Being a Real Estate Agent Can Be a Huge Advantage

A lot of investors say being an agent is a mistake if you want to invest in real estate. I disagree. I save money when I buy or sell, and I get more deals. I also think it gives me credibility. I saved more than $300,000 in real estate commissions last year because I am an agent. I also got more deals because I can pay more for other houses than non-agent investors, and I can act much faster than other investors.

The reason I save so much money is I make a commission when I buy and save a commission when I sell. I also am able to act much faster, which gets me more deals. I also have access to the MLS, which gives me more-accurate comps and allows me to value houses more accurately.

59

Two Houses on the Same Lot Do Not Equal Twice the Value

Two houses for one! Seems like a great deal, but two houses on one lot can be a problem. Lenders may not want to finance two houses; zoning might not be correct for two houses; and many buyers don't want two houses. Be careful when buying two-for-one deals unless it makes sense as an income property.

Often, a property with two houses is worth less than a property that has one house! if the zoning is right and the property's best use is multifamily, it could be a good deal, but remember that two are not always better than one!

60

Real Private Money Is from People You Know

True private money is an amazing tool for flipping. It comes from friends, family, co-workers, or other investors. There are no fees, no appraisals, and easy approvals. Don't get confused by hard-money lenders claiming to have private money.

Don't be scammed by people on Facebook offering $10 million dollars at 5 percent interest. They are not a real lender and will steal your application fee. If it sounds too good to be true, it most likely is.

61

Always Get Everything in Writing when Working with a Partner

First, make sure you need a partner. Many people partner up on a deal not because they need a partner but because they are scared to do it alone. Some of the biggest problems come from a partnership with no written agreements or clear idea of who does what, especially with friends or family. The best partnerships usually involve a silent-money partner and the operator. No matter who the partner is, make sure everything is in writing!

62

Meth Houses Can be a Disaster

We bought a meth house in 2003. We did not know it because the home was occupied. The guy got busted for cooking meth, and then it burned down.

Many houses with meth labs have to be completely gutted. They have a very distinctive smell and other signs as well. Many meth houses are registered with the city or state. If your alarm bells are going off, there are tests to see if it is contaminated. If you buy a meth house, it may need to be completely gutted if the contamination is bad enough. It also may need just a light cleaning. You need to test it to see how bad it is and what is needed. Each state also has different guidelines for what needs to be done.

63

Always Use a Real Estate Agent to Sell a Flip

I own a brokerage and save so much money by being an agent. If I did not have my license, I would still pay an agent to sell my houses. You get better marketing, better negotiating, better contracts, and the house sells for more money.

On the other side of it, some of my best deals come from for-sale-by-owners who don't know how to sell their house. They don't know how to price it or how to negotiate, and they chase away most buyers who want to use an agent. If I was not an agent, I would still use an agent to sell my flips because agents are worth it and more than make up for the cost of their commission.

64

Local Banks Can Be a Great Source of Funding

I have used a local bank to fund my flips for years, some at 5 percent interest and 1 point. You need more money down, but they're a lot cheaper than hard money. Not every bank will do this, and you may need to have proven yourself with other deals before they will consider it. However, it can be great financing.

Most banks will want to see investors who have some experience flipping, so you might have to use other financing until you can get in good with a local bank. You also may need to talk to many banks before you find the right one with the right programs.

65

Always Make Sure the Jobsite is Safe

I had an addition removed on one house, and it left an eight-foot deep hole in the ground. One reason I never used that contractor again was he had no fence and no markings for the hole for weeks. Always make sure any hazards are well marked or fenced off. Notice how new construction sites are almost always completely fenced.

There should be no broken windows, ponds, pools with water in them, or any other hazards. Make sure the site is safe!

66

Saving Money, Not Spending It, Is the Key to Flipping

Many people think real estate will solve all their money problems. You need money to be successful in real estate, even as a wholesaler, and especially as a flipper. Saving money, creating a budget, and being smart with cash is so important. The more money you save, the more successful you will be.

Sometimes you need to fix your money problems before you start investing in real estate instead of expecting real estate to solve your money problems. If you can't save a dime, you may need to work on that before you jump into real estate.

67

Make Sure You Check the Heat in the Winter

We are in Colorado, and it gets cold. We always check all our houses for heat and get the sprinklers blown out in October.

You cannot rely on your contractor to do it. I checked one property last week where the heat was off, even though it had a crew working there. If your house has no heat, make sure the property is winterized so the pipes don't freeze. One of the best ways to do a lot of damage is to leave the heat off, causing the pipes to freeze, break, and flood the house.

68

Don't Fudge the Numbers to Make a Deal Work

It is really easy to convince ourselves a bad deal is a good deal if you are desperate to buy. I have fudged the numbers in the past on houses that I should not have bought. It rarely works out well when you are lying to yourself.

There will always be deals out there, although they may not come right away. Sometimes, passing on a house is better than stretching the numbers to make it work. We tend to get deals in bunches. We will go a month without any and then have 4 in one week. Do not stretch the numbers because you are getting desperate.

69

A Team is a Wonderful Thing

Many people try to flip houses all on their own. They do the work themselves, find the deals, try to sell it themselves, etc. There is only so much one person can do. The right team can help you do more, make more money, and give you more time. I did 26 flips last year because I had a team.

If I was doing this all on my own, I would go crazy. I would forget half the things that need to be done, and I would not be making nearly as much money. I could not go on vacation or spend as much time with my family. Do not be afraid to hire people and get help!

70

Paying for Materials Can Be a Great Way to Save Money

Most contractors shop where it is easiest for them, not where the best deals are. They are not concerned with saving money but with what is convenient. Some even mark up prices. Many contractors will also ask for a lot of money up front because they have to buy materials.

If you buy your own materials, this solves many of the problems. We also get cash back and a ton of great deals by having a managed pro account at Home Depot. We can also buy in bulk and save money.

71

Text2Confirm is Awesome

I talked about buying materials for contractors. I did not mean investors should be going to the store, buying materials, and delivering them to the contractor.

The investor should be paying for the materials and letting the contractor pick them up or take delivery. Text2Confirm is a wonderful program for this at Home Depot. You give Home Depot the credit card, and they text you when a contractor is in the store ready to check out. You can approve the purchase with the text message. It saves so much time, and you can review all the purchases online.

72

A Line of Credit Is a Great Way to Fund Flips

Lines of credit are cheap, and you only pay interest when you use the money. They are a great way to expand the business. You can get a line against your personal house or rentals. If you need money, look to yourself first!

The line of credit is used against the equity you have in real estate you already own. If you have $100,000 in equity in your personal house, you may be able to get a line of credit for $90,000. When you use the money from the line of credit, you pay interest on it, but when you are not using the money from the line of credit, you will not pay interest on it.

It is much easier to get a line of credit on a house you live in than on a investment property. Many banks do not like to give lines of credits on rentals you own, and some have mentioned it is not even possible in some states. In those cases, it might be good to look into a refinance.

73

Beware of Haunted Houses and Dead People

In Colorado, you do not have to disclose any deaths in a house, but other states are much different. Make sure you know the laws!

In New York, there was one case where disclosing a haunted house was required. However, the owner had advertised it as a haunted house for years, which the courts decided had given it a negative stigma in the area.

Every state has different laws for disclosure, so make sure you know what you are and are not required to do!

74

Always Get a W9 From Your Contractors and Subs

I just had an electrician ask if he could be paid 20% less if he did not have to fill out a W9. That means I may not be able deduct that expense if I ever get audited. So, it costs me 30 or 40 percent in taxes.

We get a W9 from every contractor and sub before we pay them. If we pay them first, getting that form signed is like pulling teeth. Before you make that first payment, get a W9!

75

Why Won't My Flip Sell?

One of the biggest mistakes I see is, when a house flipper goes over budget, they try to make up for it by raising the asking price. Then, the house doesn't sell, the costs pile up, and things go from bad to worse.

The market decides what a house is worth, and we can't change that. Don't price homes too high since not only are you adding to the costs but your money is stuck in that deal. I actually let Nikki, my project manager, price my flips because I know she is not emotionally tied to them like I am.

76

Take videos and Pictures of Every Flip

Not only is it fun to see the before and afters, but they can be used for many purposes.

I use before-and-after pics and videos to market myself on Facebook, YouTube, and Instagram. I have gotten private money and more deals by sharing what I do.

The pictures and videos also come in handy with contractors. Sometimes, there is a dispute about what was done or what needed to be done. The video almost always shows the truth.

77

The Key to a Successful Flipping Business is Doing More than One at a Time

It is tough to make a living flipping one house at a time if that is your main source of income, not just because the profit isn't huge but because you don't get paid for months at a time.

The trick is getting multiple flips going at once and keeping the money turning with quick sales. I have 14 going now, but earlier this year, I had 22 at once. The easier a flip is, the more money we tend to make on it!

78

Flipping Really Cheap Houses Can Be Tough

Flipping expensive homes can be tough because all the costs are higher. In many cases, the margins make up for those costs.

With low priced homes, the margins may not ever be high enough to flip. If a home will only be worth $50,000 after the repairs and you have to spend $30,000 fixing it up, is there any price worth buying it at? Make sure you are running the numbers and they make sense!

79

House Flipping Will Not Fix Your Money Problems

Many seminars and coaching programs promise huge results without needing any money or credit.

The truth is it is really hard to flip houses with money, let alone without money. Making money without spending money in real estate is not impossible, but it usually does not involve flipping. These programs are usually teaching wholesaling but call it flipping to sound sexy.

If you have no money, sometimes the best thing to do is work on your money habits before you jump into real estate. Save money; look for ways to increase income; and look for ways to cut spending. Those habits will be needed in the real estate business anyway.

If you really want to be successful in real estate with no money, understand you will have to outwork 98 percent of people and be willing to go way outside your comfort zone.

80

An Owner-Occupant Flip Can Net Big, Tax-Free Profits

The owner-occupant flip can be a great way to get started in real estate or make a lot of money as an experienced investor.

If you live in a home for two years, you most likely will pay zero capital gains taxes on the profit: up to $250k for an individual or $500k for a couple. There is no other investment that gives you a tax free profit!

Not only can you make tax free money, but you can also use low-down-payment owner-occupant loans. Just remember you have to live in the house. If you get an owner-occupant loan and do not live there the specific amount of time in the loan docs, which is usually a year, it is considered fraud.

I have done this a couple of times, but I wish I did it more when I was younger and it was easier to move!

81

It Is Really Tough to Flip Houses in a Different Market

House flipping can be very challenging in your own market but even tougher in another market. Running a flipping business takes good agents, lenders, contractors, and a project manager.

I have seen investors run successful flipping businesses from afar, but they had great project managers who ran everything. The flipper also spent a lot of time in that market setting things up.

I would also be wary of companies that claim they will flip for you if you buy the houses. I have not heard many good stories come from those, but I have heard many bad stories.

82

Insurance Can Be Expensive...and Tough to Find

Getting homeowners insurance on house flips can be tough. Many insurance companies won't insure them. Those that will tend to charge a lot more than on regular policies. Foremost is one company that will insure them, and most insurance companies have access to their policies.

We have had some companies that specialize in house flips try to get us on board. They offered builder-policies only, and we had to get separate liability insurance. It was a major hassle.

83

Goals Are Almost as Important as the Work

If you have no goals, how do you know you succeeded? Setting goals is one of the most important parts of any business.

I set a goal to flip 30 houses in 2017, and I flipped 26. I set a goal to make $100,000 a month flipping in 2018. I fell short of that goal as well.

Am I mad? Did I fail? No! The point of a goal is to help you do better than you would do without the goals. The goals did exactly what they were meant to do: keep pushing me all year long.

84

When Do You Need a Building Permit?

I don't like getting building permits. It is a pain, can take forever, and adds much more work to be done. However, in some cases, you have to get them.

==If you are doing an addition or major remodeling, you need one. Most electrical work requires them. Structural changes also require permits.==

This is one reason we try to stay away from huge remodels. We still do them, but we are careful what towns we do them in as different towns have different permit rules.

85

Do Not Be Scared of Your Contractor

Working with contractors, when they seem to know everything and you appear to know very little, can be intimidating. That does not mean they are always right or you cannot learn from them.

It is okay to question why work is done a certain way. It is okay to tell the contractor you want it done a different way. Sometimes, they do what is easiest and not what is best. You also may know what will help a house sell better than them. You could also be wrong and look like an idiot. That is okay too.

You should be in control of the project. Many of my contractors want to go crazy with repairs, and we have to reel them in sometimes. It does no good to spend so much money on repairs that you can't make a profit.

86

Make Sure the Doors and Windows Are Intact in the Winter

Many contractors love to leave the doors or windows open when working, even in the winter. They don't pay the heating bills, so they aren't that concerned about it.

Open windows or doors can kill your heating bills. There are enough costs on flips without adding unnecessary costs.

One contractor claimed we had a leak in the propane line because we were using so much of it. Turns out he had two windows wide open in the dead of winter all day and night.

Make sure you don't have any broken windows or doors and the contractors know to conserve heat.

87

You Can Flip Houses in Any Market

Many people say you can't flip houses anymore because the market is so good. That simply is not true. We flipped 26 houses last year and may do more than that this year.

It was almost easy to flip houses after the last crash. But, flipping houses is not easy. People who say you can't flip now may not know anything about flipping. Foreclosures are not the only way to get a deal. In fact, I have not bought a foreclosure in over a year.

The key to flipping is getting a great deal, and there many ways to do that in many markets. We have been flipping for 16 years in good, bad, and stable markets. If you know how to find deals, you can flip.

88

I Don't Care About the Schools or Crime

This may seem crazy, but I really don't care about schools zones or crime rates when flipping. I care about what comparable houses sell for. Comparable houses will be in the same school zone and have similar crime rates. They will tell me how much the house is worth.

I also am not going to judge what constitutes high crime or a bad school. I know what I want for my kids, but other people may want something totally different. Comps tell the story, not my personal bias. .

89

Lowes and Home Depot Offer Awesome Military Discounts Year Round

Home Depot and Lowes both offer a 10 percent military discount year round. There are some restrictions on the discount if using it with other discounts or clearance items. From what I could understand, Menards has a very limited discount that may or may not be available depending on the store.

If you have never looked into a VA mortgage, it is one of the best loan programs available for owner-occupied military personnel. It offers zero down and mortgage insurance.

90

The Average Purchase Price of My Flips Is $200,000 and My Average Profit Is $36,000

My average profit has always been around $30,000 per flip. That is after financing and all other expenses. Lately, the profit has gone up slightly as prices have gone up.

I never use a blanket rule to figure profit like a certain ROI or the 70-percent rule. Each house is so different with and involves different budgets. The profit margin I am happy with varies from deal to deal.

I am happy making $25k on some deals, and on others, I want to make $50k plus. It all depends on the costs I will have, the risk, and the rehab.

91

Save Time by Not Attending the Closing with the Buyers or Sellers

When you become successful, one of the toughest challenges is finding enough time to do everything you want to do. I am always looking for ways to save time.

One thing I do to save time is I almost never attend closing with the buyers or sellers. A closing can take an hour in some cases. I can sign my side of the deal in 5 to 10 minutes. This morning, I signed closing docs on two houses I am selling and on one house I am buying in less than 30 minutes. If I would have attended all those closings, it would have taken hours in driving and waiting.

Look for any way you can to save time!

92

Water Is One of the Most Destructive Forces

One of the biggest causes of major damage to a house is water, and that's not just from flooding!

The main reason foundations fail is from water. It could be the grade sloping into the foundation, no gutters, or even a high water table. Most water problems can be fixed easily. If they aren't fixed, it can cause tens of thousands of dollars in damage.

I have bought many houses with water issues, and usually, they are much easier to fix than people realize. You have to make sure you fix them!

93

Buying in Bulk Can Be a Great Way to Save Money

I started with storage units but then bought a small commercial shop. It is so nice having space for bulk purchases from Home Depot. We can buy 15 vanities that are on clearance at a time. We can buy thousands of square feet of laminate and 8 rolls of carpet.

Home Depot calls us first when they have sales because they know we can take whatever they have. We have bought 15 vanities at once before for less than $50 per vanity because they had them on clearance. We also have supplies available and do not have to wait for shipping on some items, which can lengthen the repair process and cost us money.

It is also a nice place to store a car or two if you run out of room at home like some of us have.

94

Is There a Best Time of the Week to List a House?

Many people want to wait until the spring to list their houses. When flipping houses, I do not wait to list them, except for very specific holidays like Christmas or Thanksgiving. There is no guarantee a house will be worth more in the spring than it will be in the winter. Prices could drop, and there also might be 50 other people waiting to list similar houses in the spring. You may have no advantage by waiting, except the extra carrying costs and opportunities lost by not turning your money quickly.

I once waited to list a house until after Thanksgiving. I think that you want as much attention as you can get when first listing a house, and listing right before Thanksgiving, Christmas, or other major holidays can limit that attention. Real estate agents will not be paying as much attention to new listings or be as willing to show houses on holidays.

I also avoid listing houses on a Friday evening because many agents will not see the listing until Monday. I want my houses listed in the morning or early afternoon and preferably not on a Friday (although that always seems to be the day they are ready).

95

Help Appraisers Out!

When flipping houses, we often run into appraisal problems. We have very nice houses that may be priced the highest in the neighborhood.

When the appraiser schedules their appointment, we send them comparable sales and a list of repairs we have made to the property.

This can help an appraiser understand the market better. We also tell them if we had multiple offers. It does not prevent every low appraisal, but it helps.

96

FHA Appraisals Stick with a Home for 6 Months

There is a huge difference between FHA and conventional loans. FHA appraisals stick with a property for 6 months. If an FHA appraisal comes in low, you can't hope for another appraisal to come in higher with a different FHA buyer. You must find a buyer using a different loan type.

If you are using a conventional loan, you may be able to order another appraisal or use another lender who will be able to order a new appraisal.

97

Don't Forget to Shovel the Walks and Mow the Grass

One thing that is easy to overlook is shoveling snow on your flip projects. The city can fine you, and you don't want someone falling and suing you because you didn't shovel. You also want everything nice and clean when the house is for sale. We have a landscaping company set up to shovel snow whenever there is a storm so we do not have to think about. We just make sure they know all the vacant properties that will need it.

98

It Is Possible to Challenge a Low Appraisal

When flipping houses, appraisals often come in low because we are trying to sell the nicest home in the neighborhood. There are ways to prevent a low appraisal, which I talked about in a post from a couple of days ago. You can also challenge a low appraisal.

If the appraisal comes in low, talk to the buyer's lender and see if they will challenge it. You will need at least 3 comparable sold properties that were not used in the appraisal. They should be similar to the subject property, and you need reasons why they should have been used instead of the other comps. Or, if you can find a blatant error in the appraisal, that is a huge advantage. We once found the appraiser measured the square footage incorrectly.

The lender can then ask the appraiser to review the new comps or mistakes, and they may or may not raise the value. We have seen some appraisers stick with a horrible value and others raise their value 20 percent or more.

99

You Do Not Have to Completely Remodel Every Flip

Some of our best flips involved us making minimal repairs. We replaced a roof, repaired some windows, or made other repairs that would be required by FHA. This allowed us to sell to an owner occupant without doing a full remodel.

By doing this, we reduce the time and cost to repair. We can also price the property below full retail. This makes the buyer happy because they are getting a deal and can make whatever cosmetic repairs they want.

100

The First Offer You Get Is Often the Best Offer

If you get a good or great offer on your house, take it! Being greedy and trying to squeeze every penny out of a deal can chase the buyer away and cost you money. Waiting for multiple offers is tempting, but if they never come, you may lose your best buyer.

If you get a subpar offer, it is fine to counter them or wait for good offers, but don't ignore a good offer in hopes of getting even better ones. Some buyers don't like to play games, and if you don't respond right away, they may look elsewhere simply out of spite.

101

Flipping with a Partner Is One Way to Flip with No Money

Many people want to flip houses, but they don't have any money. Banks won't lend money to people who have not flipped houses. It becomes a catch 22 where you can't get a loan to buy a flip, and you can't buy a flip to gain experience without a loan.

Using a partner to fund the flip is one way to get in the business with no money. It is not easy, and you will have to work very hard to find a partner willing to finance the entire deal. A typical deal has one partner finding the house, getting the work done, and selling the house, while the money partner provides money. The split is often 50/50 in this situation, but it can vary greatly.

To attract a partner, you better know what you are doing and have a presentation ready to blow them away.

102

Conclusion

There is much more to flipping houses than what is in this book. This book is all about tips and tricks to help you succeed in the house-flipping business. My book *Fix and Flip Your Way to Financial Freedom* goes into much more detail on how to find, finance, buy, repair, and sell house flips.

I also show before and after videos of just about all of my house house flips on the InvestFourMore YouTube channel. I also have many more videos offering advice on rentals, showing my rental properties, and expotic cars.

My blog https://investfourmore.com also shows the numbers on every flip we have done in the last few years. It shows the numbers on all of our rentals, and we have hundreds of articles on how to flip, how to buy rentals, being a real estate agent and much more.

You can also follow us for daily posts on the InvestFourMore Facebook and Instagram pages.

About Mark Ferguson

I have been a licensed real estate agent/broker since 2002. My father has been a Realtor since 1978, and I was surrounded by real estate in my youth. I remember sleeping under my dad's desk when I was three while he worked tirelessly in the office. Surprisingly—or maybe not—I never wanted anything to do with real estate. I graduated from the University of Colorado with a degree in business finance in 2001. I could not find a job that was appealing to me, so I reluctantly decided to work with my father part-time in real estate. So many years later, I am sure glad I got into the real estate business!

Even though I had help getting started in real estate, I did not find success until I was in the business for five years. I tried to follow my father's path, which did not mesh well with me. I found my own path as an REO agent, and my career took off. Many people think I had a huge advantage working with my father, and he was a great help, but I think that I actually would have been more successful sooner if I had been working on my own, forced to find my own path.

Now I own a real estate brokerage. I fix and flip 20-30 houses per year, and I own 20 long-term rentals. I love real estate and investing because of the money you can make and the freedom running your own business brings.

I started InvestFourMore.com (a blog) in March 2013 with the primary objective of providing information about investing in long-term rentals. I was not a writer at any time in my life until I started this blog. In fact, I had not written anything besides a basic letter since college. Readers who have been with me from the beginning may remember how tough it was to read my first articles, with all the typos and poor grammar (I know it still isn't perfect!). My goal has always been to provide incredible information, not to provide perfect articles with perfect grammar.

The name "InvestFourMore" is a play on words, indicating that it is possible to finance more than four properties. The blog provides articles on financing, finding, buying, rehabbing, and renting out rental properties. The blog also discusses mortgage pay down strategies, fix and flips, advice for real estate agents, and many other real estate related topics.

I live in Greeley Colorado, which is about 50 miles North of Denver. I married my beautiful wife Jeni in 2008, and we have twins who were born June of 2011. Jeni was a Realtor when we met in 2005 but has since put her license on ice while she takes care of the twins. Jeni loves to sew and makes children's dresses under the label Kaiya Papaya.

Outside of work, I love to travel, play golf, and work/play with my cars.

Want to Learn More?

If you enjoyed this book and are interested in learning more about real estate, you may be interested in my other books:

- How to Build a Rental Property Empire
- Fix and Flip Your Way to Financial Freedom
- How to Buy a House
- How to Make it Big as a Real Estate Agent
- The Book on Negotiating Real Estate (co-written with J Scott)
- How to Change Your Mindset to Achieve Huge Success

I also write new articles on my blog https://investfourmore.com all the time and have many resources for investors and agents on the site. I have hundreds of videos on the InvestFourMore YouTube channel as well. We shoot videos of just about every house we buy, and I have been buying close to or more than 30 properties a year the last few years. You can also follow me on the InvestFourMore Instagram or Facebook page where we post daily.

Made in the USA
San Bernardino, CA
28 May 2020